AF571935

THE BODIES WE WERE LOANED

THE BODIES WE WERE LOANED

by Maria Terrone

THE WORD WORKS
CAPITAL COLLECTION
WASHINGTON, DC

First Edition
First Printing
The Bodies We Were Loaned
Copyright © 2002 by Maria Terrone

Reproduction of any part of this book in any form or by any means, electronic or mechanical, including photocopying, must be with permission in writing from the publisher. Address inquiries to:

The WORD WORKS
PO Box 42164
Washington, DC 20015

Cover art: Photo by Daniel Hugos, 2000

Book design, typography by Janice Olson

Library of Congress Control Number: 2001096196
International Standard Book Number: 0-915380-49-8

ACKNOWLEDGMENTS

Grateful acknowledgment is made to the editors of the following publications, in which many of these poems first appeared, sometimes in slightly different versions:

Atlanta Review, "For a Brother in Cyberspace"
Blueline, "Beets"
Crab Orchard Review, "Garden of the Impossible," "The Last Summer Job," "To Hold This Splendor," "Faith"
Dogwood, "With These Words" (Second Prize Award, Poetry, 2001)
Heliotrope, "What They'll Say in a Thousand Years"
Kalliope, "Two Women Waiting"
Literal Latté, "Night of the Comet"
Notre Dame Review, "The Men on the Wall"
Passages North, "Strawberries"
Pivot, "Gulls and the Man," "Links"
Poet Lore, "Inside the V.A. Dictaphone Typing Unit, Division of Outpatient Psychiatry, 1969," "Lipstick" (from "Flesh That's Signed")
Poetry, "Madame Curie," "Drifts," "Ghost Frescoes"
Potpourri, "Under Lexington Avenue"
Rattapallax, "In the Still Jade Water of Noyac Bay," "A Question Between Waking and Sleep"
Rhino, "You'll Burn in Hell, the Pretty Woman Said, Smiling"
Southern Humanities Review, "Firewalking Through November," "From the Other Side"
Southern Poetry Review, "The Passage"
Sou'wester, "Imagine the Obscene Caller"
The Spoon River Poetry Review, "The Sum of Her," "Loose Powder" (from "Flesh That's Signed"), "Motel Room," "Swagger"
Sycamore Review, "The Poet's Surgery," "Among You," "Bob in His Valley"

Verve, "Vesuvius"
Web del Sol, Editor's Picks, "The House of Juliet," "Heart Murmurs"
Wind, "Saturday Night Music"

"The Trial" was awarded the 2000 Elinor Benedict Prize in Poetry from *Passages North,* and "In Standard Time" received the 1998 Allen Tate Memorial Award from *Wind.*

"Gatherings" appeared in the *Emily Dickinson Award Anthology* (Universities West Press). "The Idea Is To Have Hearts on a Shelf" appeared in *Divided Again,* the Clones Poem Contest chapbook of The Edmonds Institute.

I wish to express my heartfelt appreciation to Enid Shomer and Louise DeSalvo for their unflagging generosity, encouragement and friendship, and my gratitude to Kate Light and Deena Linett for their insightful comments as this manuscript was taking shape.

For my husband, Bill,
and Nanette

CONTENTS

IN THE STILL JADE WATER OF NOYAC BAY

inky-green seaweed drifts by,
each clump mysterious and complex
to me as a word of Asian text.
What is the sea trying to say?
You read too much into things,

is what others observed about my search
for meaning—the truth beneath
a chance meeting or casual phrase
that may, after all, mean nothing.
But today I can't stop brooding

over the buried Chinese emperor
(guarded, the paper said, by six thousand
life-size terra cotta soldiers) and the peasants
haunted for centuries as a fierce red eye
or scowling mouth thrust through

the field's clay crust. Now a lone
swimmer appears; only his arms are visible,
breaking the water's opaque surface
like the arc of the letter *O* rising
again and again. Nothing churns up

from the deep but the white moiré
scroll of his own motion,
and I pick up my pen, awed
by such eloquence, the body's
unequivocal language.

THE EXAMINED LIFE

I'm looking to hire a private eye to spy
on myself, someone invisible equipped with a scope
and insight. I want a pro who'll float
above my shoulder, taking notes, ascribing
motives, but mostly I want an hour by hour
record of every texture, sight and sound—the solid
facts. *She wore a 30's chiffon dress and vivid*
pink lipstick Saturday. She bought sunflowers
and every few hours that night her face cropped
up beside them, bothering the pane like a pebble.
I want a full report on my life without double
talk, words like 'hunger' or 'joy.' So if my diary stops
and mind shuts down, I'll have proof, delivered
daily: *Here it is. She came and went. She lived.*

GARDEN OF THE IMPOSSIBLE

"No stone becomes immutable before its final consecration."

—Isamu Noguchi

I have brought my father in spring
to Noguchi's walled garden
where sinuous sculptures
of granite, basalt, travertine rise up,
defying expectations

of stone—sun-hoops shining
red and black, coiled marble cobras,
a teetering helix that probes
the possibilities of air.
But these dancers

are hard, old as the earth.
Winter lingers inside my father.
He walks stiffly, pausing to trace
taut curves of skin, following
cleavage to the heart within.

I watch from a distance, wishing
his craftsman's hands recall
what his mind may no longer grasp—
that even the most obdurate
matter can bend to a man's will. I'm hoping

those hands, now so soft, remember
metal's bite, then its easy yielding
as he bent and soldered new life forms:
exuberant copper swirls I pinned
to my breast, tin knights who dueled

across our table, the xylophone he played
off-key. Now the sun aligns above his head
and granite becomes a black mirror
that reflects my father back to me.
If Alzheimer's is a slow hardening,

whose art will make his brain agile
as these stones? If Alzheimer's is a tangle,
why can't every twist
be made straight, here, in this garden
of the impossible?

GULLS AND THE MAN

Shocking to me: the solitary man
perched high on a girder of the Whitestone Bridge,
until his yellow hard hat bolts
into sight, his wind-burned face,
legs that ride a wedge between sky and sea. Closer,
and more startling still:
grasping a tiny whisk broom, he dusts the ledge
with a motion delicate and precise—
a jeweler brushing a watch's gears.

The gulls must be curious too,
about this creature with a head
the color of the sun,
rooted in air but flying with them.
They shriek, circle and dip,
brushing whorls against sky
to match his lifted fingertips.

I suppose their keen eyes
detect the dust motes as they fly
from his prickly straw, swirl
in currents above them and come to settle
in the nearly invisible spaces
between their own ruffled feathers.

As the man and gulls recede
from sight, then merge to gray,
I can only wonder if this man
will be riveted tomorrow
to jackhammers and resistant earth.

And his fallen gulls:
reborn as feather dusters that hide
in the hard-to-reach corners
of hardware store shelves, dirty
before they even begin work.
Or dyed the jewel tones
of Fabergé eggs—the fabulous
plumage of Easter hats
shivering a little, in shame.

THE PASSAGE

(From an undated photograph of New York City subway construction workers)

1. Boy Among the Sandhogs

The laughing boy, perhaps fourteen, crouches
inside the open legs of the surveyor's tripod
like a child playing under a table.
Mud, tactile as the remains
of a fudge sundae, rims his lower lip, the eager
cavity of mouth. Blackness
nearly scoops his cap away,
but from its tweedy blur two wisps
of hair escape, wet as tea leaves
we can read on his fragile brow.
Above and behind, four tight-lipped men clutch
the tripod, knotted veins tugging the length
of their outstretched arms. The men anchor
their weight against the force
of compressed air, the angry river pushing
back. The boy can't see them. He can't see
how close the stone vault curves
to the men's hard bodies
like a woman about to embrace
her beloved, or how their restless eyes search
four different directions for an exit.
As if unformed, the boy's hands
and lower body do not appear. But his face shines
atop his slim stem of torso like a new bulb
streaked with earth.

2. The Surveyor

In the heat of the tunnel, he is the one
who wears a deep, stiff collar
and the startled look of a bird
banded, squeezed into a cage.
He's retreated to shadow but the complex rigging
atop his tripod lists forward
like a clipper ship straining to set sail,
blown on the labored breath of men.
The sandhogs hold still as death,
posed for the tiny explosion that will seal
them here before us, but something unnamed
has been set in motion. You can see it
in the surveyor's collar, bright
vortex of a gathering darkness.
Seconds later he'll collapse
his equipment and disappear, leaving the men
alone in this unimaginable void,
shoveling, blasting, inch by uncharted
inch in their passage beneath the bedrock
of a new land.

3. Four Men Under a River

They've arrived. Survived
the Atlantic, that oily black cur growling
day and night like the ship's engine
at their ears. Survived the deepest
deck heaving human muck, the awful
undertow of yearning that pulled
them clear across the sea. They've arrived,

landing in this cave below a river, on the jagged
shores of an underworld reserved for men
like them. The work boots of the man up front
tilt oddly, as if struggling for a toehold,
high laces like rope ladders climbing the darkness.
Entering the airlock to descend
the caisson, did they know that hunger
would return to consume them?
That with every breath,
they would once more feel the crashing
ocean in their heads?
They've arrived, shoulders sloped
as if the men themselves were ballast—
a gritty mass laid down at the foundation
of what will surely rise.

MADAME CURIE

Even through her cheap boots she felt
something shift below the earth,
and her skin tingled, a thousand tiny bombs

exploding in on through her fingertips,
belly, hips, the very roots of her scalp.
Even picking mushrooms, she saw the glow

worms and fireflies throb brighter
as she neared. When her mother died,
she gave up her bed to boarders, stoked their last

embers, boiled their *pirogi*. She tended rich
children, charges that circled her
like a planet's moons. Even gravity stopped

trying to hold her down. Science whispered
in her ear, stirred her, pulled her across every border
to Paris and Pierre. How they pulsed,
huddled together in the lab with a box of radium,

watching rays burst free and split
into alpha, beta, gamma. How they beamed
at the Folies Bergères, all those legs

rising and falling like happy electrons.
Thin, squinting men in top hats heaped prizes
on them. Even when a streetcar's wheels

rumbled by to claim Pierre, Manya pushed on,
an engine doing its work. She rigged x-rays
on vans to see the wounds of war, killed tumors,

burned skin off her fingers. She glowed, she believed
in the triumph of good. Even when her great heart
stopped pumping, needles jumped beyond their scales.

"THE IDEA IS TO HAVE HEARTS ON A SHELF"

—Biomedical engineer quoted in a newspaper

In the fullness of time (a decade, they predict)
and money (5 billion, give or take)
and scientists' damned
hard work (the calculation of minds that knew
from the getgo the heart's eternal power
to raise funds, rally even the wary;
in short, its public relations value
over liver, kidney and spleen)—

hearts will beat on a shelf.
It could have been otherwise. Left alone,
stem cells might have chosen
another path, bloomed
as muscle or vein, but were induced
in laboratory light to this—a pump organ
tuned to nonstop celebration.

Soon they'll appear in a glass showcase,
labeled, plumped up like a pasha's
rarest pillows. Take one down—carefully, now!—
and feel the satin flutter against your skin,
insistent whisper of a heart wanting in,
the rush of your hidden
city, its roar and raging heat, the wild
dark needed to become human.

INSIDE THE V.A. DICTAPHONE TYPING UNIT, DIVISION OF OUTPATIENT PSYCHIATRY, 1969

I felt like a voyeur at my gray steel desk,
wired from ear to tape recorder, recorder to foot,
bound to the veterans of Vietnam who confessed
to night sweats, panic, drunken bouts, brute
scenes erupting in their stricken minds
like bomb-blasted earth. Their words bored
through my ears all day and spread inside,
shrapnel that tore at the heart of a girl
who hadn't yet known sorrow, men or war.
When I couldn't hear them, I pumped a pedal,
retreading the same scorched ground. The force
of demons propelled some voices—fierce as metal,
urgent as sex. But some whispered, and I saw faces
pain-twisted, men still pinned to a ravaged place.

THE LAST SUMMER JOB

Today, riding the el alongside the factories,
I saw through a broken window a single blouse
suspended in the hot breath of a standing fan.
Arms strangled or hugged as it twirled
white and dazed on an industrial hook,
pulling me back to when I was nineteen, waiting
for my life to begin at the end of that season,
the end of each day.

I hunkered down to that last summer job
before I married, tapping keys, filing requests
in drawers, my foreshortened motions
defined by wall and wall and wall, held
inside the squat, windowless bunker
of the Hunt Chemical Company.

Each day I waited with the other women
in a concrete yard for Hunt's hired man
to drive us to a place we could never find ourselves,
bumping over cratered streets and past the droning
staple factories. Our morning murmurs trailed off
as he pushed deeper, and we became lost
inside ourselves. I was nowhere
I could name except wife-in-waiting,
so I wore a blindfold against the dreariness,
peering at next summer's wedding
and the following fall, unwrapping the years
one by one like bridal gifts from their tissue cradles.

Each day, he left us without a word
and I pushed open the door to a way station.
There must have been phones,

I must have called my love often,
the dial turning like a wheel of fortune,
I must have spoken to friends and family.
But I remember only shy exchanges
with a bookkeeper, a woman thick and faded
as a ledger, skilled at reading the heart's fine print.

I punched no clock but heard every minute
edge towards my future. Eight hours times
five days times ten weeks, I tried to keep my love's face
before me, to remember that my morning captor
would lead me out and I would become
every woman ever saved
from a burning ledge, a capsized raft,
the bottom of a well.

VICTORY'S REMNANTS

> "Every conceivable remnant, in every possible shade and hue, turned and squirmed in the thin morning sunlight."
>
> —*The New York Times*, May 8, 1945

The morning before VE Day, a rumor
that began as a dream's half-formed
whisper floats through the city's canyons,
slips past filmy windows to move down
the rows of the garment factory workers,
repeated from one seated woman to the next
like a long, unbroken chain stitch until
what lies before them is complete,
and dazzling:

The war is over.

Over and over they try on the words,
now standing up on tiptoes,
arms stretched high as they can reach
as if to test joy's strength, its durability.

The work is done.
What need now for these remnants,
scraps of unfinished business?

The women fling until their arms ache,
then lean into the air above Seventh Avenue,
watching the fabric reel:
cuffs that won't know wrists,
a half-sewn pants leg open at the seam
dancing past felt swatches verdant
as some patch of land the soldiers never found.

Muslin strips sweep across sky, not skin,
past square fields of flowered cotton
that bloom mid-air.

The war is over.

The youngest nearly tumble out,
tracking the path of taffeta
that parachutes down, ecstatic,
to vanish within the human tangle.

FIFTY YEARS AFTER

We were spellbound for two hours, so shaken
we had to write down his words
as soon as we reached our hotel.
Then we held each other in the terrible heat
that was England that summer,
fifty summers after Hiroshima.

He had boarded our train in Bath,
heading for a London military affair,
his big dog Sam at his feet.
He had cheated death
so many times during the war,
he still grinned now at 78—his weight
when freed from the camp in Burma.
From a battered briefcase he pulled
medals, papers, a postcard to his mother
with his message encoded in Pitman,
Keep smiling, the strange angled lines
an affirmation buried
among captors' official lines
announcing his death.
His mother stared at the card for hours
until suddenly she saw—even next door
they heard her scream, "My Smiler's alive!"

To escape the heat earlier that day
I sat in a Norman church
under windows of stained glass
and recalled that people once believed
in the healing power of that light.
I imagined coolness washing
over me like the river Jordan,

spring's first rain, the spirits
my mother used to soothe my fevered brow.
Instead light flung its fury
through every shade—crimson
the Divine King's robe, blue
the Madonna, the gold
of archangels's wings—
each shade a flaming tongue
that branded me speechless.
Dutiful tourists, we forged on in what I came to understand
was our crucible—
plodding heaths that whirred
the high, nearly soundless pitch of heat,
entering treeless Cotswold towns exposed
like open wounds to the sun's blistering
glare. That whole summer, I found no refuge
except inside my lover's arms.

I worked to build their railroad,
tree trunks strapped to my back,
pulling my shattered leg along
with a rope. Once I was beaten
for not bowing low enough.
But I'd known magic tricks from childhood,
and they amused the general.
He kept me there when my buddies
were shipped to their deaths.

I first escaped death
when a grenade blew up my lorry,
hurling me just beyond the fire,
then in our makeshift hospital,
when soldiers rushed in, plunging bayonets
through the men stretched out on cots.

I escaped death by malaria
because I sewed blankets together
and slept inside my stifling hood.
I escaped death by starvation
because I ate the maggots
that others picked from their infested rice.
Despair stalked me, growling
Give up. *But then I'd picture myself*
back in Kent, sitting with my mother and girl
at the kitchen table—they felt closer
to me than the death I lived with.

At home in America, a lavish book,
"The Great English Country Homes,"
had dominated my coffee table.
Within, the greensward
of West Wycombe Park—an Arcadian dream
to fall into whenever insomnia struck.
But those lush and lordly lawns were burned
brown, the ponds around the mock
Roman temples clogged with monstrous fronds.
Everywhere, fire engines howled; I shut
my eyes, and they raced towards my dreams.
Heat and traffic fumes colluded, poisoning
the anemic blue veins of sky, people
bent wheezing below. Health alerts
filled the airwaves, the elderly and weak
warned to stay indoors.

The A-bombs had been dropped, the war
was over, but we didn't know it.
For 20 minutes, we stood
before the firing squad waiting
to die.

In pub and hotel, Hiroshima
replayed: the same stunned orphans stumbling
through rubble, their skin raw peels
that kept unfurling. The stones
of Parliament buckled, undulating molten
along the Thames' blanched banks.

I was invited to Japan recently
and treated like a hero.
I went into classrooms and talked
to the children—I even ate
with some of my guards. Some people here
say that I dishonored the memory
of those who died.
But I blame no one. It was just the war.

Our train reached the terminal
and we shook hands with Fergus Anckorn,
retired business teacher,
member of the Magic Circle of Magicians,
father, widower, son of England.
We stayed rooted to our seats
as he climbed down into the crowd,
a thin old man who still moved with ease.
I couldn't stop thinking about heat and war,
why some men are burned
with the tattoos of hatred,
others cauterized to forgiveness.

THE MEN ON THE WALL

Brawny men on the wall hoisted iron, their steel
muscles rippling. Painted before the second war
by WPA artists, the mural celebrated work
and freedom, cities rising bolt to beam, the red-
blooded and able-bodied. At 17, I felt strong, armed
for my summer job at the VA, ready to hear

and transcribe the words of vets—not conquering heroes,
but mental prisoners of war. Tapes awaited in a steel
box, but I was brooding over the one-armed
elevator operator on the way up who wore
medals against his heart, and the headline I read
in the lobby: *Mekong Bombed Again—The Work*

of General Westmoreland. They say a woman's work
is never done, and mine was to hear
the cries of drowning men who thrashed in the red
well of my ear. Each day I was linked by cords of steel
to a Dictaphone, a Pandora's box of secrets—war's
aftermath, terrors that rage long after the arms

rust. Each day, the pain: head, neck, arms
and fingers convulsing till I went numb from work;
the tapes in my out-box rising, casualties of war
stacked like two-by-fours. Did the other typists hear
the same kind of stories? Did they have to steel
themselves as I did? Did the women also blush red

in pity and shame for men who fought the Reds
and survived, only to jab needles in their arms
to join the dead? I glanced around, saw steely
eyes fixed straight ahead, feet like pistons working

a machine. Some veterans complained of hearing
voices; they said the doctors' drugs helped but wore

them out...No one in my unit ever talked about the war.
Our ballroom-dancing boss flounced up the rows, her red
dress a swirling flag. Even now I can hear
those tapping heels, see her gather tapes in her arms,
then waltz out of sight. When I remember that work,
I picture the hungry, stalking wolf who steals

the red-hooded girl. That fall, eaten alive by war, I begged
God to hear me and work two miracles: melt steel
arms and save the men who now speak from the black wall.

UNDER LEXINGTON AVENUE

This tunneling train shudders
into stillness, and I am a sleep-
walker held in the danger
zone between thought and dream.

A creature unseen stirs nearby,
then slithers up a pole and strokes
my hand. Recoiling
I grasp a spot so low
down I can hear my vertebrae crack.

Waiting below ground with strangers: a breath held
too long under sea, an anchor pulling
deeper. Feelers find my fingers
and strum them to a chill,
as if my hand were breaking
down to nail, knuckle, synapse; as if my
self were deconstructing.

The train groans awake, tips
me backwards into torso. In sudden
light so many legs
and arms akimbo,
so many hands, whose
fingers? whose face?

II

HEART MURMURS

Meaningless, the doctor says.
He can barely hear the sound—
really a tiny click—or make out
on the screen the out-of-synch
ventricle flap that shuts
an instant too late.

Harmless, he pronounces,
removing the sticky prod,
and I think of street people
murmuring
to no one in particular,
the steady, background sound
of a machine that doesn't want
or need attention,

while others may murmur
for months or years
and then without warning,
attack,
furious that no one came close
to listen.

FOR A BROTHER IN CYBERSPACE

In your land-locked state
your valley sealed by snow,
I think of you bound in place like the crook
of a broken arm, the hard crust
of Vermont winter a permanent cast,
you shriveling inside, puckering to nothing
like the peaches of last summer that lay unnoticed
on your land. If you were really broken—
if you skidded off Loop Road, say, spun into a ditch,
or began to fracture
in ways I couldn't see,
you know I would leave New York
to scrawl graffiti up and down your limbs:
"I was here," and being there,
talk you back to yourself.

We should write letters, you said
one summer stopover here, sipping wine
with me in the garden dark. I nodded, knowing
the mountains would soon enclose you,
unable to foresee the day your thoughts
would vault across the space
between us and drop on my desktop
with a toy trumpet's fanfare.

Twice, three times a day I open
the picture of an envelope, viewing
from my twelve-inch window
a life lived on the back roads.
You send reports of snow depth, wind chill,
a collapsed bridge that left you stranded—
your words icons

of danger that make me shiver
until they're banished with a stroke
to another, safer place. The trumpet calls
once more and I see you as you were just seconds ago,
hunched in flannel at your basement desk,
hooked index fingers tapping
out each letter—my brother adrift on a floe,
chiseling SOS on ice.

WHAT IS TAKEN

From the hospital hallway,
I see my mother before she sees me,
a little at a time.
So hard to take in the small shocks
of hair, face missing its makeup,
once-restrained flesh now ungirdled.
Her bandaged right hand, huge
as a prizefighter's, crosses
her chest as if she hopes
to ward off blows
or swears to tell the truth.

"Agony," she says, shaking
her head. "The local wore off
and I could hear them sawing
inside my hand." I can't imagine
the pain able to crush
my mother's stoicism, her belief
in the power of her own will.

Opposite her bed, a wall-mounted box
is crammed with disposable gloves: limp
white fingers touch the glass
that contains them. Beyond us,
the whole East River is broken up
and wrapped in the gray gauze of dusk.
A barge wheezes past the window,
horn escaping in short, hard gasps.

It will be months
before her hand can lift a fork
or thread a needle's eye.

THE POET'S SURGERY

For Enid Shomer

When you told me they removed
one of your ribs and fused

its pulverized dust to your spine,
I imagined Eve asleep, mind

and body stilled by poppy fields.
(In this poem, not just your name is planed

down to archetype—you're bone of his bone,
every limping woman who tries to walk alone

in the garden.) A white-robed god
stands beside your rent body,

triumphant arc of rib
held high, as if he plans to give

back to Adam what was first his
and undo you. But stops, because they'd miss

the brilliance of words that sing
fluttering from your tongue

like birds of paradise. And because you can
conjure an apple so true to its ideal, man

knows the sweet taste of poetry
and why he must have it, too.

AT THE KNIFE-SKILLS WORKSHOP

"First you must choose the proper tool,"
the chef proclaims, lording

over his empire of carbon steel.
He raises the twelve-inch knife,

then tours the room checking thumbs
for proper placement. "Be sharp!" I command

my faltering mind to become like the blade
I hold, but I'm thinking of tools

besides these knives—the files and pens,
picks and awls that people take up,

along with their daily bread. I'm thinking
of my cousin, who lies now in a hospital bed,

fixing a customer's car. He's crawled
out from his head and underneath

the chassis; all day long, hands no longer
veined with grease gladly twist the air.

BEETS

I think they must be very old,
holding fast for years in a tight cold place,
escaping the scythe through sheer
homeliness.

They wobble on my cutting board,
big awkward knobs smelling
of rain-soaked soil, sparse hairs
trailing from grayed, misshapen domes.

When I boil and slice them open
I find a tree's concentric rings
closing into one tiny secret core.
Peeled, their skin is smooth as a youth's
and radiant.

I love the way they yield their essence
with such ease,
surprising me the way my gashed knee
surprised me as a child.

We are lively, they say, vibrant,
not at all what you thought.
Let us mark you with our brilliance,
spiral scarlet over your fingers,
stain your hands with our sweet ageless blood.

I want to carry their stain for days.

SALT FOR UNCLE CHARLIE

Like Apicius, who preferred death
to ingesting a bad meal, my uncle,
forbidden salt, declared, "It's just not worth it."
A month later, he was dead—betrayed

not by his bounteous heart, but his cells,
suddenly massed against the prospect of a bland
life. My uncle, happiest in the kitchen
patting his dough, felt condemned, denied

even the condemned man's banquet.
But the last time I saw him alive,
a sheet lay tucked under his chin
like an oversized napkin. Reclining

in that hospital bed—eyes half-closed,
lips curled—he seemed to me suspended
in that ecstatic moment between the scent
and taste of his own homemade feast as,

drop by drop, his veins sipped
saline clear as eau-de-vie.

TWO WOMEN WAITING

In a kitchen, hungry
for news of his accident, the women
pass the time with a carving knife
and a bursting squash.
Better to save than watch it rot,
each thinks but does not say.

They sit face to face across the table
and pass the knife to and fro.
Wordlessly, they slice,
pushing till the rind
yields perfect curves.

Silently, they make their preparations,
sprinkling oil, applying spices,
striking a match for the oven.

Will he ever taste this?
each thinks but does not say.
The room swells with heat.
Under a frozen-starburst clock,
these hands move as one.

THE SUM OF HER

She strides in, a striking figure all eyes add up:
taller than most men on the train, curves

slick in shiny stretch pants. A long knife scar
rides her left cheek like a skid mark

on a dangerous road she once took, and yet
she stands erect, proud and self-possessed

as a statue of Venus. So hard to solve this problem
of division, to see how one bisecting line

white as fear, sharp and clean as a shard
of ice can brand her as more or less

than a woman. I'd expect her downcast,
hunched in a corner, or out for vengeance, slashing

men to nothing with a swift razor-blade
glance. Shouldn't one with that face fall to pieces?

Instead serenity flows from bottomless eyes
focused on infinity—she's a Hindu goddess,

pure form honed by Picasso, bursting all frames
of reference. Nothing of this woman coheres,

nothing about her is easy—like someone we know
but can't name or a puzzle that's just too complex,

she's studied from all angles, then subtracted
as every pair of eyes turns away.

YOU'LL BURN IN HELL, THE PRETTY WOMAN SAID, SMILING

and the man who had dared to steal a look
across the subway aisle hooted. A bible small
and square, forbidding as a padlock on a jewel
case lay over her trim lap. *The good book*
tells me you're damned because you seek
the body's pleasure. Her trumpet voice blasted fallen
souls—him and every one of us. I was enthralled
by this prophet in flame-red lipstick,
but the man's laugh was just a grin now, a gag
pulled tight against his whitening skin. *Die,*
devil, she hissed, watching him struggle to lift
his heft from the well of a plastic seat. When he sagged
back, destroyed, she leaned into him, a perfumed bride
of Christ, tract in hand, face anointed with bliss.

IMAGINE THE OBSCENE CALLER

alone on Saturday night
picking up the phone in his single room
or tiptoeing upstairs to dial
on the au pair's private line,
or hunched inside a phone booth,
turned away from the ice-floe glare
of a gas station floating on a black road.
Imagine him wherever he may be,
his heart freeze-dried, breath shallow
in the dead space before the rings begin.
He connects:

his congealed blood flows
at the sound of a woman's greeting,
a neutral hello reserved for purveyors
of credit cards, magazines, political surveys,
his knotted tongue uncoiling
with the slick, free offer he makes
over and over into a mouth-
piece riddled like a sieve,
his words falling
through the holes into a silence
so thrilling, every click is a kiss
on his burning ear.

AMONG YOU

(The man known as the Ely Avenue slasher was never found.)

Sometimes the rain
seeps into the subway
and streams down the filthy
tiled walls days later
like an icon's unexpected tears.
They stream for the Ely Avenue
garment workers,
the ones who had bodies like slugs
and worthless faces like gray rags—
invisible if not for the lacing of scars
I gave them 20 years ago, here
in this station. Once a crude

drawing of the face
they imagined was mine appeared
on hundreds of subway stanchions.
Police fanned out, handed flyers to fools
who took them home in their pockets
and purses, as if I could be read
like a newspaper in lamplight.

Sometimes while crouched on all fours,
weeding my lawn on a bestial
summer day, I think of how salt thirsts
for itself, how my sweat mingled
with theirs, seeping through pores
and wounds—all the fresh openings
I made—taking them unaware,
the way toxins disappear
into rivers, earth, the food you eat,
your own bloodstream.

THE TRIAL

1. Sitting in a Pastry Shop the Day After Jury Duty

Afternoon light glazes a row of cakes
topped with chocolate shavings
that curl like a woman's lashes.
A piped-in concerto celebrates
peace and plenty,
but I'm thinking of hunger and crime,
how emptiness

can drive a body to the edge of the world,
how a French-speaking African
working a donut shop's graveyard shift
alone, stood at a single greasy window
facing the street where
a young American, wild-eyed to feed
his habit, waved a silver gun.
You know the rest.

2. What Luck Means

Just like Las Vegas.
No windows or clocks to distract
from the wheel's turning,
this high-stakes game.
The clerk spins names in a wire cage,
calls them out like roulette numbers,
puts us in the box
for questioning. One man says
his son was strangled
by a stranger he happened upon
and took home—*Dismissed.*

A woman whispers about her step-daughter
stabbed to death in a schoolyard
brawl—*Excused.* Our cars stolen,
houses burgled, distant cousins mugged—
You're the lucky ones, we're told.
The reporter's tape keeps rolling out,
a jackpot of words. A wall
of white marble climbs behind the judge,
In God We Trust, letters a mile high,
shimmering like fool's gold.

I'm sworn in as the last juror,
then the room suddenly clears
the way it does in a Western
when a bandit sweeps into the saloon.

The DA steps up for his opening statement,
leans in, takes a swing. For a split
second, two strands of spit stretch
like bars across his lips.
He shifts again:
the bars implode, and a bird
on his tie takes flight
before settling inside a fold.

3. Games of Chance

Two die roll towards each other
on lush green felt.
They collide and in that instant
before they bounce apart,
we're born;
another game of chance begins.

The defendant:
being born.
Being born in the projects.
Waiting in jail
a year to be tried.

An eyewitness:
pregnant—waiting for the one egg
out of millions to grow;
folding sheets one February night
in a laundromat
when an armed robber
walks in—that man, over there.

A liquor store owner:
survived Auschwitz *(Objection!)*
ordered to crawl
towards the back of his store,
gun barrel inches from his skull,
handcuffs clamped over the mark
left by his eighteen-thousand-dollar Rolex,
strapped now to a stranger's wrist.
I picture him, palms stuck to the floor,
each tick loud inside himself
like the nervous pulse of a bomb
marking time.

4. Last Words

The machine clicks,
and the strips of paper fold

back and forth on themselves,
thousands of words mounting.

Thrust, counterthrust.
I recall the defense lawyer's signet ring
flashing like a knight's sword, the blades
of opposing voices that clanked
and crisscrossed, voices sharpening
to slash the other's body
of evidence.

And in the last moments of that last
day, the silence.
Faces turned our way, grave
as the always-empty gallery.

We find the defendant
Guilty. Guilty. Guilty. Guilty.

The man we judged begins to moan,
a sound like rumbling released
from the earth's hot core.

The reporter hoods
her machine—only words
are recorded here.

5. The Verdict

At home after the verdict, gasping
as if the air had been flung down
and bundled over me by the secret police
of an equatorial country, I escape

to stand on the sidewalk and absorb
the balm of a late spring
twilight. Nearby, a man stoops
to peer at the pavement

and then hurries away. As if pulled
by a rope, I find myself staring
at a lizard-like creature—banded
brown and white, still as death

and as watchful,
armored tail tapering to a hook,
tiny horns almost fetal
but ancient as a fossil, too.

A shiver crawls
up my spine, lingering
on each vertebra, as if
the idea of evil has emerged

perfectly formed from a nest
of philosophers' scrawl, pushing through
their age-old, prickly questions
about good and evil, justice and mercy.

I know, in my bones, this creature
has traveled miles, inching over the space
of years so that it can cling
to my doorstep
and look me in the eye.

DRIFTS

Your footsteps
through our garden's deepest snow
end abruptly,

as if you had vanished to a flake,
your atoms rearranged
to crystal. Strange, that the life

of perfect symmetry you sought
would come to this:
your measured motion forward

subsumed by the angles and planes
of drift, each step that marks
your absence advancing

a theory of chaos. How could you
disappear this way?
Our stone bench, so lean in summer,

now pushing up on padded haunches,
hawthorn tree twisting
towards the impression you left—

like them, I have nearly split in two,
straining to erase
the souvenirs of your passing.

WITNESS

The sea grasses in the plovers' cove still whisper
about what they saw. Tall as you and I,
they're doubled over now, their grief
a hushed sound like water trickling

inside a grotto. A week ago a man
came to this beach on his day off and lay within
a burrow he dug. Eyes shaded, ears plugged
with music, he back-floated on sleep's blue
cushion, when a ranger's van climbed a crest
of sand, then plunged down on him. I know this

only because you told me; you were told
by Miguel, who used to cut
the dead man's hair. Nothing grows
here of course. Nothing solid rises

from the sand to mark the place
of death, its ever-shifting hills
and valleys. I lie here with you
thinking of this, watching the sea plow closer
and a wide-eyed congregation of gulls
that faces one way, immovable as stones.

A FALLING CADENCE

Last tatters on the maples,
the eye wants to fill in the new, raw spaces,
assign a Rorschach meaning.
I look at the leaves as if they might speak,
but like swallowed words,
they furl back on themselves.
Some try to break away, tumbling out
in quick succession, then down,
the rhythm of a sentence half spoken.

For days I woke to a vague sadness,
rain like gray fingers thrumming
at my window: *it's time.*
The mind can play tricks.
But not this morning at a diner,
when I sat transfixed, watching my empty
glove mimic my living body.
It lay sideways on the counter,
black leather puckered over the missing
ridge of knuckles, fingers curled palmward
as if they could not, or would not,
unclench. I gripped
the steaming coffee in both hands and stared
as the fingers slowly straightened,
then tipped back to lie flat,
and still. Not such a long time before absence
asserts itself.

Now the jagged leaves, scattered
like jigsaw puzzle pieces,
are sun-blurred to a single, tawny field.

The leaves still attached to this world flare gold
like the tongues of orators holding forth,
their trunks stately pedestals
that hold them up,
even as they speak their last words.

SATURDAY NIGHT MUSIC

Our conversation clicks like castanets
of insects celebrating a summer night.
We're once-scattered friends landed
around a table, caught up in a swirl of time,
the jubilant rhythm of *remember when*
until our one-note song stalls and dissonance stops
us cold: after sixteen years, Vincent's wife

has left. He talks about how much he loves
a certain band, driving miles to watch
guitarists pluck away the blues
from a circle of stage light calm as the moon.
His long hank of thinning hair trails
like a loosened rein.

Raf, two decades divorced, is no longer alone
but has found his way with a girl named Ariadne.
A teacher of virtual reality,
Raf says she is almost, but not quite, here with us.
I picture a wraith funneling across the heartland,
her breath the sibilance of wind through reeds.

Laura's baby is overdue,
so we rise to clink our glasses, chiming
a welcome for the one soon to join us—
the child who pounds inside the drum,
keeping his own beat.

BOB IN HIS VALLEY

After twenty years in Vermont,
my brother can name the wildflowers on his land:
Milkweed. Meadowrue.
Lupine. Feverfew.
I say each word aloud, rolling syllables on my tongue
like segments of blackberries, trying to taste
the country that pulled him away.

Last night, shocked awake in the unfamiliar
room, I thought all the stars of Andromeda
had pierced the bare pane and tattooed
my body with their blue needle pricks of light.
Now I'm a stranger in my skin
as I'm a stranger on this land, pores and pupils
big as sinkholes, taking everything in—
boulder and mold motes, flutter and flicker.

As we hike, the sun rims clouds with brightness,
yellow highlighter in a dark, dense text
telling me *Remember this—your brother's face luminous*
with pride, this walk together after a long absence.
True to his calling, Bob tallies up
the four dozen stakes he drove to mark the borders
of his woods; below us, he says, 15 bird feeders
have made the meadow a haven
for finch, hummingbird, and mourning dove.
I smile to think of them scribbling mischief across a sky
once blank as a new page in one of his ledgers.

Here and there, shadows spill their inky stains
over his weathered boots, my silly sandals—
lazy shadows that now leap

to the sound of wingflap, as if a sheet left to sun-bleach
had been taken down, wrinkles snapped smooth.
Above us, a poplar is shrugging a branch,
unable to account for imbalance,
the fleeting weight it bore.

MOTHER'S HOUSE AT 3 A.M.

Foo dog snarls from his pedestal
like Cerberus guarding the portals,
while Diana, bronze-embalmed, poises,
her arrow aimed.

Your house is a temple and I a night visitor
wandering past ivory elders in repose,
jade blossoms, incense burners, cloisonné.

Everything is as you left it.

Grandfather clock, solid, upright,
went mute years ago.
His pasty moon-face glares at the pagan splendor

and me: Dazed, barefoot, I seek you
in this overgrowth of tapestry and topaz.
I light a candle
and whisper your name,
your first-born daughter, bereft.

FLESH THAT'S SIGNED

1. The Makeup Box

I'm picking the lock on Mother's makeup box,
its blue suede nap seductive
as night glimpsed through the fuzzy windows
of childhood. I'm a young girl
fingering Eve's apple, hungry to know

the origin of my world, aching for the one
thing withheld. I lift the lid—hairpins scatter
in darkness like small electric shocks—
and inhale. Powdery wisps
sheer and pink as Mother's peignoir fly away

in my breath. Once, waking as a dream
of her receded, clutching my sheet to pull
her back, I mistook pinwheels of stars
for the rhinestone swirl she wore that night
to match the flash of her made-up

face. She seemed to lean towards me
from just outside the window, her breast
sparking indigo fire. Then I felt her
cocktail dress brush my cheek, and I followed
in sleep, trailing the scent of perfumed satin.

2. Lipstick

Like an arrow, the greased point took aim
at the blank canvas of Mother's face,
hovered, then stopped short, as if space
had solidified, or fear. Always the same

morning ritual at the mirror: "Protect us all,"
she prayed, lips cracked from the cold
breath of departed aunts. Painted boldly
for the coffin, they were like malevolent dolls
who crept inside her sleep, promising harm
to come. I hunched against the icy tub
and watched Mother tighten her robe
as if the belt could restrain her alarm.
Sighing, she drew the tube into place. Then red
flowed, and all day long her lips mimed
those warnings of the dead—
not in words recalled from dreams
but in violent kisses left behind
on cups, clothes, the flesh they signed.

3. Loose Powder

Flesh of her flesh. So I am and so it seemed to me
was Mother's loose powder—everywhere,
restless particles that changed the chemistry of air
as she did. And what do I see when memories
are stirred up like sand in wind? A racing
storm cloud of energy. She hurled
into rooms, rearranging chairs, plans, even the curls
on my doll's head, then left, replaced
by a stubborn pink essence. Sometimes I'd stroke
my finger across her bureau, trying to find my name
in its cloudy face, or I'd play a game
that the top was a chalkboard and I the pupil she doted
on. But long after all the lessons on slates
were written and erased, that dust on my flesh remained.

MOTEL ROOM

The floor slants as if inclined to permanent depression.
Standing at the door you foresee

everything: the mattress, hidden like a robed patient
in worn chenille, sagging

a fraction more tomorrow—your imprint gone
but your weight absorbed;

and someone who lies behind the wall; on this side
a refrigerator, bare except

for a dented soda can. Already you can hear its hungry
shudder in the night and the stranger's

answering groan. There's a room beyond this room:
you know the mirror, scratchy as reception

on an old t.v.; the slit for used blades that will widen
by the hour like an eye that takes you in;

the shower thundering in a rusted stall. You watch
the incremental escape

of your pale body, first the right foot, then the taut
bridge of your arm extended

to grasp a towel that will abrade and scatter your dead
cells like snow over the ruined

carpet, and how you will vanish, turning
on your heels to go.

III

GATHERINGS

Behold the Bones of Man,
the bio textbook seems to say. See
them thin as threshed straw bound
together in darkness. But note
how the fingers and toes fan out,
taking the shape of a much-used broom.

Do you recall that old man who swept
the Avila cobblestones with twigs?
Does he now inhabit the Spanish air?
Your photo bracketed
two small boys who flew into his brambled
shadow, seeking the haven
of a body bent like a tree at timberline.

What is a photo but the sweeping
of an eye that can take in more
than our own? And what are we
but a heap of gatherings compressed—
not just muscles held by sinew and tendon,
but a lifelong collection of thoughts crammed
in a small room. Even our voices
the tension of two taut cords.

THAT INWARD EYE

Sometimes red eyes appear in our photos—
never when we're snapped by surprise, but posed

in our suits and silk finery, stiffly smiling,
unaware a part of us has been replaced by—what? an exiled

creature sprung from secret sockets? Like banned
cigarettes in a dark theater, red eyes burn

holes in expectations. Although we may laugh
when we first see the shots, thereafter,

we fear others will regard us a certain way:
How charming in that gown or *Such a handsome guy*—

but in a sudden flash perceived as insight:
She could flare up so quickly, though and *He might*

on occasion try to steal your date for sport.
You want to cry out, *"That's not me,"* distraught

over these leaps into nastiness, if not quite hell
incarnate. Officially? The retina's vessels

bounce blood-red from the flash, but that's science
speaking. I propose a theory of self-defense:

red eyes are vestigial stoplights to scare
off hunters; hidden eyes behind the lens that stare

a second too long, as if we could be known pinned
flat to paper, picked up later, examined.

A QUESTION BETWEEN WAKING AND SLEEP

If
awakening to the grave
face of a predawn sky,
a granite slab incised
with rain, I try to conjure
the features of the one I love
but find they've been erased,
like names on old headstones
that have become the stone's
blank face;

and if
memories of the places
we knew were to depart
one by one, tiptoeing out
like restless house guests,
which would be the last to go—
the Alhambra of our honeymoon
or all those rooms by the sea
whose torn lace curtains
filigreed our bodies silver-blue?

ON A SUNDAY SEPTEMBER NIGHT

Through the French doors of our den
I watch you, the image of a man
framed by concentration. Articles
clipped from your physics journals
rest on your lap, and at your sockless feet
I can just discern the runes
of your mysterious discipline.
You work alone,
the steady center
of a perfect circle of light.

It brings to mind a certain painting:
an ordinary white house at late dusk
transfigured by its own glow,
suspended for one instant against the cold
of encroaching dark.

Now you are curved over papers reading
of charmed quarks and quasars and I can't
imagine what else. From just across
the glass I detect
the almost imperceptible click of decision
that crosses your face—
the flutter and fractional lifting
of your eye as you render judgment,
then the swift motion of your hands
towards one stack or another, rising
like turrets foursquare around you.

And watching your furrowed absorption,
your pure heart oblivious
to all clank and clash beyond this room,
my own heart stirs like the leaf
that scratches now at the window screen,
unheard.

FIREWALKING THROUGH NOVEMBER

If sunlight touched
the ground earlier, I wasn't there
to see. The fallen leaves are stuck
in their sullen swirl
like thoughts of a mind
that can't stop mulling over the lack

of possibilities. In the past half-hour,
they've gathered,
leaning against a gritty wall
like street-corner vagrants.
They shift in the wind to rasp
a faint protest: nowhere to go

but down. Yet the few gold leaves
that still hang on the trees
are now back-lit
to a transparency
you could pass through
not just unharmed but warmed.

Think of the word *beneficent*—
like a glance
that happens to catch
the sun's last rays striking a pane,
you hold the afterimage
until you feel you could leap

through fire, that window,
see your way clear
through anything, even a dead season.

MONET AND THE MEDITERRANEAN

"It is so beautiful here, so bright, so luminous!
One swims in blue air; it is frightening."

—Claude Monet on the French Riviera, 1888

Madness
is what Monet called attempts
to compress that light,
but in nine frenzied

days at Menton, he stopped the flight
of time, trapping moments
like butterflies
inside ten frames. I'm buoyant

here on his mottled seas,
each smudge
of sea-foam green
a stepping stone to the next,

darker shade, the day drifting
away unnoticed
like the crowds until
a guard draws near and I gasp to see

myself walking on water,
and then violet waves
are breaking, pulling
me into the deep.

VESUVIUS

On a Mediterranean day that reminds me of God
on the Sistine Chapel reaching
down and snapping sparks
between his fingers for the first time,
I am in a car
with my husband at the wheel heading
to Naples daydreaming of Pompeii and how when
liquid fire began to undulate down the mountain crawling
and clawing towards the city how a curtain
must have dropped over the sun and did
those people think
they were still asleep?

As I wonder
a tunnel swallows us.

Blindfolded we fall, hurtling
with no lights front or back
so that we do not exist, have never existed
to those fast approaching, pressing
so close we can hear their steel hearts rumble.

My husband's hands are grasping at bulges
and squares on the rented car, his hands
that strum guitars, stroke me alive,
his slender, seeking
desperate hands, and I am
paralyzed,

thinking that I may die
inside this mountain in this place
where families are frozen forever, hands reaching

across a table for a piece of bread or fixing
a sandal's loose strap, in the land of my buried
black-eyed ancestors and

just then his fingers find a knob and light,
a big, furry white dog guiding
us out and back into the beautiful blinding
Mediterranean day.

FROM THE OTHER SIDE

That first time in Italy, I couldn't get over
how well the dead and the living get along,
citizens of the same city rubbing shoulders

at every turn—the way the eyes of men
framed in wall shrines would tenderly follow
the widows who passed on their way home

with sacks of fruit almost scraping stone;
or cemetery-bound, carnations pressed to the mounds
of their breasts, engrossed in silent conversation—

as if the beloved who'd passed to the other side
sat just across a table. *Dio mio!*
the women scream, *vespas* grazing their hips.

The drivers salute with their mineral bottles.
On the label, Professore Minardi of the Turin
Science Institute affirms the water's ability

to promote a long and healthy life.
That first time in Italy, I couldn't get over
the public bathrooms, narrow as coffins,

bathed in a kind of séance light.
I feared the strange locks on those doors
and stared as I might back home

before an abstract painting, trying
to discern the secret, how all the pieces
are supposed to fit together,

bring you in then lead you out.
But I might not get out
until I'm found dead, I thought, trapped

later in the cellar toilet of a café
by the murky Bay of Naples—a tourist trap
of a place where old men shuffled about,

selling roses, scratching out *Santa Lucia*
on battered violins. A place where you expect
to pay with lira, not sudden tears

for dead relations; and only a stranger,
someone's grandmother calling
what must mean *Stay calm* from the other side

of the unbudging door, can release you,
the full, stiff weight of your body
sprung into her black haven.

THE GULF BETWEEN

Such a long time before we'd understand
the true meaning of the squiggle, that our map's
blue line wasn't a road but a river—a dead end,

in fact. But the only words newlyweds know are *alive*
and *beginning*, so we laugh as we lurch
round and round in our rented car, surviving

our obtuseness, still practicing how to shift gears.
How do you cross the border between two nations?
Years passed before we learned—first you steer

in circles, lay blame, repeat yourself for hours.
But since this is the Costa del Sol (where all couples
should start), the umpteenth sighting of a certain flower

pot enlightens: of course! we had both misread
the map! Nothing to do but spend the night
in that crazy border town. Forget *he said, she said,*

and the gulf between. For now, picture
two young travelers on one side, joined
in amazement as Iberian dogs saunter

into cafés like bachelors sniffing the air for action,
the parade never ends and, unwilling to part
across sleep's divide, we wait, wide-eyed, for the ferry.

THE HOUSE OF JULIET

Of questionable authenticity and taste sneers
the art guide to Verona. But love's pilgrims
don't care. They spring eternal in the courtyard
of the medieval *palazzetto*—an empty tomb
except for me and some bored guards. The action
is all down there. From her mullioned window I watch
the play, the blithe extras jostling
for a chance to rub the pure, untarnished breast
of bronze Juliet, graceful as a dancer
on her pedestal stage. Here come the young
Romeos, lips caressing the mouths
of cell phones. Broken off from a tour group's knot,
two Asian girls weave towards her,
hair streaming like black banners
above the silk sails of their jackets. An old woman
steps up and pats the breast as if wise
to the ways of rising bread.
Not done yet, her cupped palms say,
forgetting the end and its taste of ash.
Her husband's shaky hand spirals
in slow motion, a last wish
he can't stop making. After every homage,
the crowd cheers, a faith in love natural as breath,
and I too sigh for love's outpouring: all the undying
declarations, the bright, heart-to-heart names
written over cobble and brick, trash can and telephone,
blanketing these walls almost to the balcony,
where they lie together,
a field of buds forever suspended in April.

GHOST FRESCOES

Basilica of San Zeno Maggiore, Verona

A chubby fist and wing
float free, severed
from the landscape of human affairs.

Below, a barefoot saint
seems to straddle acres, beaming
casual self possession, the divine

right to stake eternal claim—but
in the space between
both legs, a third intrudes,

last remnant of a man fading
to white dust. Nine hundred years ago
this wall was his. Reduced

to a toehold, he now spites
the fourteenth-century arriviste,
holding his ground with the ghost

of what he was. The saint remains
oblivious. Centuries sweep
around him like planets' rings;

the church's wheel-of-fortune
spins rose light
through plague and war.

Yet so vivid
are his blue and russet robes,
he glistens—a refugee

from a sun shower
who's arrived dripping wet, an idea
fresh from the brush of his maker.

TO HOLD THIS SPLENDOR

Last day in Venice: already the future tense
rides these ripples. I see myself drifting in a trance

back home tomorrow, a woman who searches
mirrors for *La Serenissima.* I'll touch

the face there, as if blind, but the glass will say
nothing. Insomnia will pull me down to my gated

garden, where I'll pace in the jaundiced
haze of anti-crime lamps, the latticed

metal fence dragging its shadowed chain.
In tomorrow's light, I won't see flames

like cats' eyes at *palazzi* windows or the raised
Easter chalice that pressed all eyelids closed.

Maybe it will have rained, so the moon
is drowning in a dozen piddling lagoons,

and beads of stagnant water cloud the blood-
shot red azaleas. In a few hours, night's gloved

hand will lower a veil over the face
of this arabesque city, and the last traces

of silver will dull, then blacken.
Already I can see my photo album—

memory's reliquary stored in a felt sack,
exposed for viewing on cold dark

days. But I'm still here, San Giorgio's pillars
float so close, I can almost hold their splendor

in my hands, and I'm like a cup once blighted
by a harsh indifferent air, now dipped in light.

AFTER HUNDREDS OF RISINGS AND WANINGS

For Bill, on his birthday

January: your moon-
washed face
white
between your temples,
silver
after hundreds of risings
and wanings, the constant
revolution, dreams
in and out
of retrograde. You were
never a passing phase.
Though I've seen
your dark side, I return
to you, your face still
not full
even at fifty-two
but more hollow now
below the cheekbones,
the restless hazel eyes
I love
like two explorers
seeking
the Sea of Tranquility.

STILL LIFE, LAKE CAZENOVIA

Waiting by my window at the inn I wonder
how long the earth can pause, fixed
in this frame: boats stripped of sails
moored at the opening of twin evergreens

heavy as theater curtains. Only a slice
of scene: clouds tacked to stillness
against a resin sky; on water unbending
as glass, a white V rigid in the wake

of a phantom vessel; each sparrow painted
on its branch, even the whorl of feathers
motionless—just as you were yesterday,
crouched aching before a cornfield's

shadowed green. Minutes swelling
to the drone of cicadas, you held yourself,
watching through a lens for the instant
that sunlight might strike a match
inside the picture you held.

OBLIVIOUS

The doctor shows me on film
where I hadn't known I broke:
a line fine as thread that wanders
across two seams.
How shrewd, the bone
knitting and mending
on secret overtime. Later I learn
that scientists are growing
bones and skin in a dish,
the details of genesis

laid bare. But I'd prefer
to be oblivious
of the lives beneath my skin—
not to recall that veins bulge
with the rush of eager blood
or ponder the load
brain circuits bear,
the flippancy of flawed cells
that can hold
the whole self hostage.

CELL LIFE

Exploring the source
of the word "cell,"
I find it springs from hell and hiding:
from *helan* (Old English), *to conceal.*
No wonder it was hell
to hear the doctor say mine
were "mildly atypical," hiding
their true nature and intent.
So the test bears repeating—but not yet.

I conceal fear that multiplies
and divides by the minute
with the typically mild behavior
of a woman at midlife who must wait.
Just as cells perform life's fundamental
functions, I dress, cook, mouth
sounds—the routine motions
of a body trying to ignore the jail of itself.
But here is my narrow bed where the hours

stretch out and stay, the shaky night
table weighed down by the heavy
inspiration of survivors' books.
I awaken cold and pass the days
like a vagabond who hugs a wall,
hoping she won't be seen.
Three years ago I was sure every stranger
could see through to the blur
at the heart of me

cast by squatters "of unknown origin"
who had slipped inside my breast.

I imagined a cluster of radicals
plotting a takeover,
captured unaware on film in their hiding
place. When time revealed they meant
no harm, every cell of me leapt, freed
from living hell. Now I wait,
once more, inside my secret.

FAITH

In the church vestibule I pass
the monitor that registers the bodies
of the faithful as gray
flickers, a second of ash
on a screen, and heave against the doors.
At 3 p.m. no one else is here but saints,
corporeal in their sandals and robes,
carrying staffs, books, painted bouquets,
their kind faces cracking
as if they too know
how it feels to come apart.

Wedged into the fingers of St. Jude
is a hand-printed prayer, a paper bud
curled so tight, I feel its plea
for a miracle tug the back of my throat:
cure the cancer, kick the habit—the ineffable
longing of a stranger's words alive
on my own tongue.

Days later, the hand holds instead
a shriveling rose stem.
Petals lie scattered about
like small, white-robed monks,
backs arched to heaven,
faces pressing stone.

LINKS

Dad sets down the scrabble board
and begins to play,
shaping words he sometimes scrambles aloud.
He doesn't talk
much lately, but he never was a raconteur.

Like a reader of Dickens, I longed for installments
to explain for me
the tumult of his life: orphanage years,
cleaning tables at West Point,
bandaging war wounds, winning, then losing
a scholarship because nights
he ran an elevator and days slept through class.

It's my mind that wanders now, trying to excavate
the pieces of who he is
or was. Oh how I want to pluck
from this jumble between us a nugget:
hard, glittering, impervious
to decay and the garble
of tongue and memory.

We play in silence, but his young voice
carries far: I hear him read my storybooks aloud,
sing forties tunes around the house,
argue for the underdog. Back and forth
we place our letters, joining
one unspoken word to another
until nearly all of the spaces are filled.

WITH THESE WORDS

For Dalio Rotondi

1.

My father at 20 crouches in the back
of an army truck that rumbles
through Normandy, Poland, Czechoslovakia.
At night he props himself up in a field tent,
bandages from his medic's training
rolled at his side, and when the other privates leave—
for the canteen or town, for a smoke,
a whiskey, a woman—my father takes out a pen
and begins to write to the girl
he met just months ago.
The paper flutters from the wind that reaches
through the tent's open flap,
and when he seals the envelope, he feels, maybe,
he's dividing himself in two, sending
the secret part airborne, away from
the rest of him, left exposed on a foreign front.

He began in friendship before the draft,
I deeply cherish your good will,
first words formal as new shoes,
hinting at early friction:
Don't apologize! I hope
we'll reach a better understanding
of each other as time goes by.
A few letters a week become one a day,
essential to my father as breathing.
Then a hundred letters, thousands
of words gathering in new terrain:

Though there may be noise and confusion
all around, reading a letter from you
lifts my heart with an intense joy.

My father is taut and slim.
In the cold shower every morning,
the words form in his mind
and make a warm mist there. He lives
on the words he thinks, his body burns
them up as he writes them down.
Love is a fire that must be nourished
or it will die.
He sits alone in one makeshift shelter
after another, says he hears music
and laughter far away.
My darling, because of you, I can stay away
from dances and temptation.
He mops the floor of the dispensary
and later, reaches into corners
to erase any doubt: *I know*
I'll make a good helper around the house.

The letters to his sweetheart bulge
like pockets stuffed with cash.
They accrue on her bureau, tilt
four shopping bags, swell two hatboxes.
They fill her head with their growing weight.
She is 20, too, a practical nurse,
a practical person, but the letters, steady
as a heartbeat, win my mother's love,
just like in the movies.

They'll be stored for decades
on a high closet shelf inside a valise,
blanketed by hundreds of photos

of their future selves and children—word
made flesh.
Beside the valise will lie marriage papers,
guarded in a steel box against fire.
But these letters, tamped down with a ribbon
and once the fire itself,
are today a smoulder, golden edges curling up,
reducing to ash.

2.

The ribbon is thin blue satin,
color for infant males.
For how long did my father
not have a name?
His birth certificate says Baby Boy.
In the letters, he writes of present and future,
not of the father who died
in his infancy, or the mother of seven who tried
to run the lumber yard alone,
dead a few years later.

Today he still can sign his name
in over-careful script,
name of the man who made his own name,
a life, me, with his words.

These days my father's words lag
like misaddressed mail. Sometimes they seem
like feathers floating just out of reach,
and he must travel a great distance in unknown
lands to retrieve them. He makes jokes
and simple puns, but speaks mainly in silence;
can't leave the house alone,
but smiles in confusion at Mother,

whose hand in his takes the pulse
of their still-beating love.

Last week, after reading for the first time
the letters she gave me,
and needing something I couldn't name,
I invited my parents to come by
for coffee. Afterwards, the table cleared:
Please hand me the...
Candy dish? Napkin? Magazine?
I offered my father word after word.
Letter? He nodded and grinned,
Yes, that's it..the letters.

I chose at random from the stack
on the sideboard, watching my father finger
the brittle sheets and slowly read
aloud. The letter was from ravaged
Rouen, where he had carried messages
to the hospital, then lost his way
through the irrational
twisting streets, trying to find the one
to carry him back to the center of town.

I passed blocks of debris, open slops,
the spot where St. Joan of Arc died,
a French soldier making a watercolor painting
of a ruined church—then all at once
I found myself where I wanted to be.
Now it is late evening, darling.
I sit here, reading your letter over and over.
Tell me you won't lose courage.

SWAGGER

Nothing grew
that shouldn't, reports the lab
after a week but my trapped,

timid heart grows, too large
to be contained by walled
chambers. Think of a hummingbird's

whir, constant as human breath,
a perpetual gasp
of amazement. What grows

is joy. Now think
of how that minute creature swells
in its white motion

like the peak of a wave flying
into air's immensity. This day
will not slink off

like all the rest. A swaggering
sun that just won't quit beats
the sky red. Clouds fat

as cherubs are speed-circling
my head—and I'm in the center
of their ring, dancing too.

AFTER YOU'VE SAVED THE BIRD

So here we are, long married, always empty-nested, bent
cooing over the parakeet that hopped on our window ledge—
homeless, hungry, broken-legged, maybe heaven sent.
Is that absurd, a flight of fancy? I pledge,
No more dramatics. But this creature who chose
you to save his life has somehow rescued me. Instead
of saying *no* (to that stray dog, to whatever lives and grows
and demands who knows what), I've found a hundred
reasons for assent. I love the way the cloud
on his blue breast pulses *yes* with every breath, his sage
countenance despite sudden life changes. He's allowed
us to repair and rename him; even in a strange cage
he sings, as if attuned to his own uniqueness—
see his black-whorled skull, just like a thumbprint, inked.

WHAT THEY'LL SAY IN A THOUSAND YEARS

Ice spikes the rungs of our fire escape
  like the teeth of a prehistoric creature
that would swallow us whole, if it could

reach through this fiercely shining glass
  into the kitchen, where we sit, together
at breakfast again. After this winter passes,

the next and the next, hors'doeuvre for a monster
  fattened on time, what will survive
of us here? I think they'll find the plainest tools—

a grainless spoon, enamel stock pot stripped
  to iron core, oxidized black skillet.
Mistaking petrified dill for pine, they'll speculate

that a grove rose at the site of the granite counter.
  "A primitive people who ate outdoors,"
a plaque above glass might say, skipping

the words passed across this wooden slab
  hundreds, no thousands of days.
But then they'll get it right: as if arranging

a hominid's scattered bones,
  they'll reconstruct the frame that held
life together: each morning, a flame,

then egg and bread, water,
  at night, oil and wine—each burned
to heat, propelling us daily from caves

of sleep, outside, into the beast's
  maw and back to the fire
again and again, to eat.

STRAWBERRIES

Close your eyes, you order, hands behind
your back: propped up late in bed reading,
I obey: my mouth opens
to ice cream, Chambord, domination

of strawberry. Then my eyes open
to you, the overflowing spoon held above
a bowl where slices float like pods
in a cool, fermenting pond. So heady,

at the end of a day that began with burnt
toast and jam, an old jar of pulp clouding
the kitchen table, the taste
of our words lingering in charred

silence. And then we went
our separate ways into the muddle
outside: stacked on my desk, half-truths
disguised as the morning news, plain

talk smeared by winks and irony—
you know, love, that read-between-the-lines
mishmash. But I'm back home,
where there's no mistaking your gaze

and my own drowsy contentment.
I could end this now with similes:
dissect the fruit to discover hearts,
cross-sections of trees, and poppies. Instead,

I'll close my eyes on today
with the sweet, simple truth
of these berries, ripe
just with the meaning of themselves.

NIGHT OF THE COMET

Once again you're excited about the sky.
This time the Hale-Bopp comet bursts
through our shell and won't reappear
until 2,400 years have come

and gone. We'll all be comets then,
returned to dust but airborne, sublime
as ballroom dancers, white tails flying.
Dust, gas, ice, water, rock—that's it,

you say, ripping aside the wizard's curtain.
Still, you marvel and so do I, watching
you carry the folded tripod in your arms,
tenderly, like a rail-thin child—

night after night, up the back steps
of our apartment house to the rooftop
where you stand shivering alone,
the lens of your eye focused

in its long exposure. And I recall
an April night—10, 15 years ago
when you drove nonstop to find
the wandering Haley's you'd dreamed of

as a child, when waiting was so much harder.
I see us then as from a great height,
the young scientist at his vigil,
eyes piercing a starless Vermont sky,

Grand Canals of melting snow, the house
behind you floating on its square of earth
and me upstairs, narcotized by country air,
turning in my lonely orbit of sleep.

IN STANDARD TIME

Only in fall these long, wrinkling
leaves become the shade
my old crayon called "flesh"—
maybe not the color of yours, but mine;
not tan, pink, or peach alone but a blend so fragile,
it almost hurts to see them. Dangling
beside the ruddy maples, they're insubstantial
as skin that wraps the very old,
tissue-sheer over a faint web of veins.
Wind that carries a top note of rain
nudges them into a huddle. Quivering
on the branch like fingers that hang from a ledge,
they seem translucent against the sky, trying
to hold on to nothing but air. What, I wonder,
am I trying to grasp, strolling with my husband
the day after we turned the clocks back,
the extra hour granted, our reprieve.

Once, early evening in this park, too many seasons
past to count, we looked up, stunned, as an aurora
unfolded like the wings of a rainbow-slicked bird.
When night emptied the playground,
we pushed all the swings into high, synchronized
arcs, laughing as they wound down slowly
like pendulums or hearts
that only will can keep in motion.
I can still hear that first wild shriek of flying chains,
the last rusty moans as the arcs flattened
into stasis, and silence. How boundless
was the sky and earth then, time
a bulging bolt of cloth we could unroll
at our own pace—the momentum

of the day carrying us playful into night,
cradling us in our sleep at noon; time
that lay easily over us like a sheet to hug one minute,
kick off the next; racing ahead or falling behind,
time that held neither loss nor gain for us,
who always woke to find our hearts
still beating inside the dewy flesh of children,
the bodies we were loaned, intertwined.

ABOUT THE AUTHOR

Maria Terrone's poetry, which has been nominated for a Pushcart Award, has appeared in many literary magazines, including *Poetry, Atlanta Review, The Hudson Review,* and *Crab Orchard Review.* Ms. Terrone is the recipient of the 2001 Willow Review Award in Poetry, the 2000 Elinor Benedict Poetry Prize from *Passages North* and the 1998 Allen Tate Memorial Award from *Wind.* Her work has appeared in the anthologies: *Mourning Our Mothers* (Andrew Mountain Press), and *The Emily Dickinson Award Anthology* (Universities West Press), as well as in the chapbook *Divided Again* (The Edmonds Institute).

A lifelong New Yorker, Ms. Terrone holds a B.A. in English literature from Fordham University. She lives in Jackson Heights, Queens, with her husband and works in public relations.

ABOUT THE ARTIST

Dan Hugos has studied at the International Center for Photography in New York, free-lanced as an event photographer, and participated in many juried art shows. His work has earned two second-place prizes in photography at the Washington Square Art Festival in Greenwich Village. Mr. Hugos, who favors landscape subjects, owns Dakota Ridge Gallery, a photo gallery in Jim Thorpe, Pennsylvania. He holds a Master's degree in Telecommunications from the University of Colorado. The cover photo was taken at a reef in Cozumel, Mexico, using infrared film.

ABOUT THE CAPITAL COLLECTION

The Capital Collection is a book signature developed by The Word Works to showcase the outstanding poetry of writers in the greater Washington, DC, area. This series is expanding with the publication of *The Bodies We Were Loaned* by Maria Terrone of New York City. The authors published in this series work cooperatively with the press to promote Capital Collection books, support other activities of The Word Works, and increase public interest in poetry.

The following individuals have contributed to the Capital Collection to make this book possible:

Donor
Christine & Frank Lombardi

Friend
Karren L. Alenier
Richard Cohen
Clare & Anthony Felice
Claudine Lombardi
Stephanie & Joseph Lombardi
Miles David Moore

Special thanks to the anonymous contributors who have also supported this book.

ABOUT THE WORD WORKS

THE WORD WORKS, a nonprofit literary organization, publishes contemporary poetry in collectors' editions. Since 1981, the organization has sponsored the Washington Prize, now an award of $1,500 to a living American poet. Each summer, Word Works presents free poetry programs at the Joaquin Miller Cabin in Washington, DC's Rock Creek Park. Annually, two high school students debut at the Miller Cabin Series as winners of the Young Poets Competition.

Since 1974, Word Works programs have included: "In the Shadow of the Capitol," a symposium and archival project on the African-American intellectual community in segregated Washington, DC; the Gunston Arts Center Poetry Series (Ai, Carolyn Forché, Stanley Kunitz, Linda Pastan, among others); the Poet-Editor panel discussions at the Bethesda Writer's Center (Maurice English, John Hollander, Anthony Hecht, Josephine Jacobsen, among others); Poet's Jam, a multi-arts program series featuring poetry in performance; a poetry workshop at the Center for Creative Non-Violence (CCNV) shelter; Master Class workshops (Agha Shahid Ali, Thomas Lux, and Marilyn Nelson); the Arts Retreat in Tuscany, and Café Muse Literary Series at Strathmore Hall Arts Center, North Bethesda, Maryland.

In 2002, Word Works will have published 48 titles, including work from such authors as Deirdra Baldwin, J.H. Beall, Christopher Bursk, Elaine Magarrell, John Pauker, Edward Weismiller, and Mac Wellman.

Past grants have been awarded by the National Endowment for the Arts, National Endowment for the Humanities, DC Commission on the Arts & Humanities, Witter Bynner Foundation, Writer's Center, Bell Atlantic, Batir Foundation, and others, including many generous private patrons.

The Word Works has established an archive of artistic and administrative materials in the Washington Writing Archive housed in the George Washington University Gelman Library.

Please enclose a self-addressed, stamped envelope with all inquiries. Find out more about The Word Works at:

http://www.wordworksdc.com
email: editor@wordworksdc.com

WORD WORKS BOOKS

Karren L. Alenier, *Wandering on the Outside*
Karren L. Alenier, ed., *Whose Woods These Are*
Karren L. Alenier, Hilary Tham, Miles David Moore, eds., *Winners: A Retrospective of the Washington Prize*
* Nathalie F. Anderson, *Following Fred Astaire*
* Michael Atkinson, *One Hundred Children Waiting for a Train*
Mel Belin, *Flesh That Was Chrysalis* (Capital Collection)
* Peter Blair, *Last Heat*
* John Bradley, *Love-In-Idleness*
Doris Brody, *Judging the Distance* (Capital Collection)
Christopher Bursk, ed., *Cool Fire*
Grace Cavalieri, *Pinecrest Rest Haven* (Capital Collection)
Moshe Dor, Barbara Goldberg, and Giora Leshem, eds., *The Stones Remember*
Harrison Fisher, *Curtains for You*
Isaac Goldberg, *Solomon Ibn Gabirol: A Bibliography of His Poems in Translation* (International Editions)
* Linda Lee Harper, *Toward Desire*
* Ann Rae Jonas, *A Diamond Is Hard But Not Tough*
Myong-Hee Kim, *Crow's Eye View: The Infamy of Lee Sang, Korean Poet* (International Editions)
Vladimir Levchev, *Black Book of the Endangered Species* (International Editions)
* Fred Marchant, *Tipping Point*
James McEuen, *Snake Country* (Capital Collection)
* Barbara Moore, *Farewell to the Body*
Miles David Moore, *The Bears of Paris* (Capital Collection)
* Jay Rogoff, *The Cutoff*
Robert Sargent, *Aspects of a Southern Story*
Robert Sargent, *A Woman From Memphis*
M.A. Schaffner, *The Good Opinion of Squirrels* (Capital Collection)
* Enid Shomer, *Stalking the Florida Panther*
Hilary Tham, *Bad Names for Women* (Capital Collection)
Hilary Tham, *Counting* (Capital Collection)
* Charlotte Gould Warren, *Gandhi's Lap*
* Nancy White, *Sun, Moon, Salt*
* George Young, *Spinoza's Mouse*

* Washington Prize winners

MORE PRAISE FOR

THE BODIES WE WERE LOANED

In *The Bodies We Were Loaned*, Maria Terrone presents us with sensuous and sensitive poems that explore the presence of the extraordinary in the ordinary. This powerful, moving book is a love song to the wounded world.

—Maria Mazziotti Gillan

Maria Terrone's scrupulously crafted, suavely cadenced poems record telling details of the quotidian world with such vividness that after a while we begin to hear "the rush" of the "hidden/city" of the heart, "its roar and raging heat, the wild/dark needed to become human." *The Bodies We Were Loaned* is a triumph of meticulous sorrow.

— Sandra M. Gilbert

Count on it: a poem by Maria Terrone entices. In her first book, expect surprises. Maria loves the exotic of now and long ago, the local landscapes of the globe. But she especially loves New York, and her splendid poems capture the joy in sounds and images so vivid, I'm there. I love all the poems in this collection.

—Walt McDonald